Are ANTS Like PLANTS?

SUPER SCIENCE

SUE HEAVENRICH

ROurke
Educational Media
rourkeeducationalmedia.com

A Division of
Carson Dellosa Education

BEFORE AND DURING READING ACTIVITIES

Before Reading: *Building Background Knowledge and Vocabulary*

Building background knowledge can help children process new information and build upon what they already know. Before reading a book, it is important to tap into what children already know about the topic. This will help them develop their vocabulary and increase their reading comprehension.

Questions and Activities to Build Background Knowledge:

1. Look at the front cover of the book and read the title. What do you think this book will be about?
2. What do you already know about this topic?
3. Take a book walk and skim the pages. Look at the table of contents, photographs, captions, and bold words. Did these text features give you any information or predictions about what you will read in this book?

Vocabulary: *Vocabulary Is Key to Reading Comprehension*

Use the following directions to prompt a conversation about each word.

- Read the vocabulary words.
- What comes to mind when you see each word?
- What do you think each word means?

> ### Vocabulary Words:
> - *carbon dioxide*
> - *harvest*
> - *landmarks*
> - *larvae*
> - *pollen*
> - *pupae*
> - *sense*
> - *tendrils*

During Reading: *Reading for Meaning and Understanding*

To achieve deep comprehension of a book, children are encouraged to use close reading strategies. During reading, it is important to have children stop and make connections. These connections result in deeper analysis and understanding of a book.

 Close Reading a Text

During reading, have children stop and talk about the following:

- Any confusing parts
- Any unknown words
- Text to text, text to self, text to world connections
- The main idea in each chapter or heading

Encourage children to use context clues to determine the meaning of any unknown words. These strategies will help children learn to analyze the text more thoroughly as they read.

When you are finished reading this book, turn to the next-to-last page for **Text-Dependent Questions** and an **Extension Activity**.

TABLE OF CONTENTS

ANT OR PLANT?

Ants don't look anything like plants. Ants have three main body parts: head, thorax, and abdomen. They have one pair of antennae, six legs, and seem to scurry everywhere.

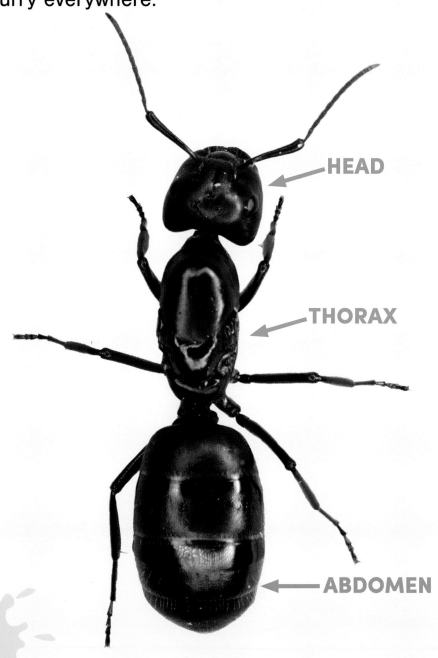

HEAD

THORAX

ABDOMEN

Plants have stems and leaves or needles. Some have flowers. They don't look like they're moving. But their leaves turn toward the sun. Their flowers open and close. **Tendrils** reach out, and vines climb trees.

They don't look the same, but ants and plants are alike in many ways. Like all living things, they need food and water. They breathe. They grow and produce offspring. Plants and ants **sense** their environment and respond to it.

FEED ME!

Water H_2O

Oxygen O_2

Sunlight

Carbon Dioxide CO_2

Plants at Work
When plants make their food, they release extra oxygen into the air. Good news for ants! Ants breathe in oxygen and release carbon dioxide into the air.

Water H_2O

When you're hungry, you open the fridge. Plants have to make their own food. All they need are sunlight, water, **carbon dioxide**, and chlorophyll.

Chlorophyll makes leaves look green. It collects the sun's energy. Water is absorbed by roots and pulled up the stem to the leaves. That's where plant cells—too tiny to see—make food for the plant.

chlorophyll

Ants are animals. They can't make their own food. So they have to find food and carry it back to their nest. Some ants eat plants. They collect seeds, nectar, or fruit juice. Some **harvest** honeydew from sap-sucking aphids. Others eat dead beetles, caterpillars, and meat from dead animals. Some even eat other ants!

Some Plants Eat Ants!
Pitcher plants have long, funnel-shaped openings. Ants slip, slide, and splash into a soupy liquid where they get digested. Yum!

Ants drink water from raindrops,
dew, or puddles. Some ants place
feathers near their nest entrance
to collect dew.

GROWING UP STRONG

Ants begin life as shiny white eggs no bigger than grains of sand. But they grow up to be strong. When they hatch into **larvae**, they don't have eyes or legs. But they have mouths. And they're always eating.

larvae

Ants Are Heavy Lifters
If you were as strong as an ant, you could carry a vending machine! Ants can carry ten to fifty times their body weight.

When they reach the right size, ants change into **pupae**. Some spin a cocoon. Finally they emerge, adults at last. Most are workers. All workers are female. They collect food, dig tunnels, babysit larvae, and care for the queen.

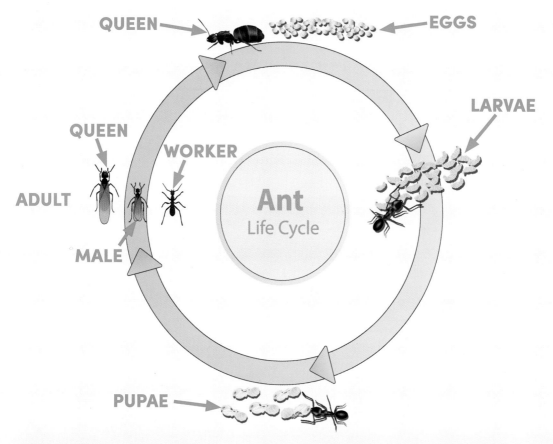

Ant larvae and pupae at different stages of maturity

Queen ants do one thing—lay eggs. Some eggs develop into new queens. They'll fly away to mate and start a new colony. Some ants are males. They don't work to help the colony. Their only job is to mate with the new queens.

Changing the Landscape
Tiny harvester ants can change how places look. By choosing which seeds to collect, they determine how and where plants grow.

Seeds may look quiet, but they're really pushy. Give them soil, water, and warmth, and they'll swell and push. They'll send roots down into the soil. The roots absorb minerals and water and anchor plants to the ground.

Weight-Lifting Plants
Plants are strong. One squash lifted 5,000 pounds (2,268 kilograms). Imagine lifting a car!

Stems reach up, toward sunlight. Leaves unfurl and begin making food. Flowers bloom, and wind, bees, or other animals carry **pollen** from one flower to another. Now the plants are ready to make their own seeds.

Plants growing too close to each other have to fight for water and sunlight. So plants find ways to send their seeds off into the world.

Travel Tips for Seeds:

Float on the wind.

dandelion

Hitch a ride.

burr

Sail the ocean.

coconut

Explode!

lupine

SURVIVAL SCHOOL

When ants are attacked, they fight back. They bite and sting. Ants release a chemical that tells other ants to come and fight. Some ants use their big heads to block the nest entrance. And some ants explode, coating the enemy in yucky yellow goo.

Got Ants in Your Plants?
Ants live in hollow thorns of acacia trees. To thank the trees, the ants chase off other insects. They also snip leaves off other plants touching the acacia.

Plant-eaters beware! These stinging nettles are covered with needle-sharp hairs filled with chemicals.

Plants can't run from their enemies. Some use bark or waxy coverings to protect themselves. Others use spines and thorns. Some plants use poison. And when they're munched by caterpillars, plants send out a warning. The other plants get the message. Then they make their own leaves taste bitter!

When ants head out to gather food, they need to make sure they can find their way home. Some ants use their antennae to follow chemical trails back to the nest. Others follow **landmarks** or use the sun as a compass.

Ant Math
Some ants can count. They calculate the number of steps it takes for them to get back to their nest.

Plants use their leaves and stems to sense light. Ants use their eyes. Plants have roots. Ants have legs. Sometimes we think plants and animals have nothing in common. But, like us, they all need food, water, and a safe place to live.

Make a Shoebox Plant Maze

Plants grow toward light. But can they use their light sense to make their way around a maze in a box?

Supplies

- bean seed (such as fava or scarlet runner bean)
- extra cardboard
- masking tape
- plastic cup
- potting soil
- scissors
- shoebox with lid
- water in a spray bottle

Directions

1. Scoop potting soil into a plastic cup. Then push a bean seed into the potting soil about an inch (2.5 centimeters) deep.

2. Spray with water until the soil is damp. Put the cup in a sunny place and keep the soil damp so that your bean will sprout. This may take a few days.

3. While you're waiting, make your maze. Start by cutting a large hole in one end of the shoebox. This is where light will enter the maze.

4. Cut two pieces of cardboard that are the same height as the shoebox and half the width.

5. Tape one piece of the cardboard inside the box on the left side, about one-third of the way from the hole. Tape the other cardboard piece to the right side of the box about two-thirds of the way from the hole.

6. When your plant has a couple of leaves, put it in the maze farthest away from the hole. Spray the plant with water. If you have to, lay the cup on its side.

7. Close the lid, tape it, and put the box in a sunny window. Every few days you can open the box to water the plant. Otherwise, keep the lid shut. Eventually your bean should find its way through the maze.

GLOSSARY

carbon dioxide (KAR-buhn dye-AHK-side): a colorless gas that is made up of carbon and oxygen

harvest (HAHR-vist): to collect or gather food

landmarks (LAND-mahrks): things in a landscape that can be seen from far away

larvae (LAHR-vee): insects in early stages of growth, which often look like caterpillars or grubs

pollen (PAH-luhn): tiny, dust-like grains, usually yellow, produced by the anthers in a flower

pupae (PYOO-pee): insects in the last stage of development before becoming adults, protected by cocoons or cases

sense (sens): to be aware of, or feel something around you

tendrils (TEN-druhls): thin, usually winding stems of a climbing plant that attach to a fence, wall, or another plant

INDEX

TEXT-DEPENDENT QUESTIONS

1. What parts of a plant sense light?

2. List three jobs worker ants do.

3. What do plants need to make food?

4. How do ants defend their colony from invaders?

5. Why do ants need to be strong?

EXTENSION ACTIVITY

Plants and animals are alike in many ways. What do you have in common with them? Create a poster that lists the ways people, plants, and animals are alike. How many things did you come up with?

ABOUT THE AUTHOR

Sue Heavenrich used to teach science. Now she writes magazine articles and books for children. Sue once spent an entire month following harvester ants and trying to trade seeds with them. Now she spends her summers tending plants in her garden and following insects of all kinds.

www.rourkeeducationalmedia.com

PHOTO CREDITS: cover and title page: ©Adisak Mitrprayoon; table of contents: ©Emine Bayram (leaves), ©DieterMeyrl (ants); p.4: ©rusm; p.5: ©Valentin Russanov; p.6: ©2017 Kevin Wells; p.7: ©bilhagolan; p.8: ©Olena Chernenko, Nancy Nehring (inset); p.9: ©Wel_nofri, AzriSuratmin (inset); p.10: ©Robin_Hoood; p.11: ©Henrik Larsson (inset), ©GlobalIP; p.12: ©tuksaporn, ©By Tomatito; p.13: ©By Pavel Krasensky, ©imv (inset); p.14: ©Sudowoodo; p.14-15: ©papen saenkutrueang, Jerry Willis (inset); p.16: ©BrianAJackson, ©Bret-Barton, ©Alphotographic, ©yanikap; p.17: ©Paonya; p.18: ©Roger Whiteway 2017; p.19: ©&#169 Phil Baker; p.20: ©Smileus; p.22: ©DieterMeyrl (ants)

Edited by: Kim Thompson
Cover and interior design by: Rhea Magaro-Wallace

Library of Congress PCN Data

Are Ants Like Plants? / Sue Heavenrich
(Super Science)
ISBN 978-1-73161-437-7 (hard cover)
ISBN 978-1-73161-232-8 (soft cover)
ISBN 978-1-73161-542-8 (e-Book)
ISBN 978-1-73161-647-0 (ePub)
Library of Congress Control Number: 2019932081

Rourke Educational Media
Printed in the United States of America,
North Mankato, Minnesota